HEAVEN SENT

HEAVEN SENT

A simple guide to communicating with angels

BELINDAGRACE

ROCKPOOL
PUBLISHING

A blessing to you as you seek the
answers for your own journey,
passions and unique gifts. The Angels
are always here to support and guide you.

Namaste, BelindaGrace

A Rockpool book
PO Box 252
Summer Hill
NSW 2103
Australia
www.rockpoolpublishing.com.au
http://www.facebook.com/RockpoolPublishing

First published in 2012

Belinda Grace.

Heaven sent : divine messages from the angelic realm /

Belinda Grace ; edited by Gabiann

Marin.

9781921878022 (pbk.)

Channeling (Spiritualism)

Angels--Miscellanea.

133.91

Cover and internal design by Seymour Design
All images sourced from Shutterstock
Printed printed in China by Everbest
10 9 8 7 6 5 4 3 2 1

CONTENTS

WHAT IS AN ANGEL?

Angels are wise, heavenly beings charged with watching over and protecting human kind. There are hundreds of angels, all of whom exist in different realms and have a different purpose in our life.

Angels will always offer help, but never force us into action. They can inspire us with new ideas or ways of doing things;

they can comfort us simply by the warmth of their presence when we are sad or alone. Angels are always around us, but few of us consciously communicate with these heavenly beings.

Many, but not all, angels, have lived on Earth. Those who haven't lived here still have the gift of empathy and relate to us very well. All angels bring a wider perspective of understanding to our lives. The vibration, frequency or dimension that they dwell in is of a higher tone.

In my experience, the number of angels with any one person remains consistent throughout their lifetime, with some angels taking a more prominent role at various times. Our angels have known us since before we were born and helped us to choose

the kind of life that would be of most benefit to our purpose in this lifetime.

Naturally, our angels are also here to help us, and many of us happily communicate with them when we are babies or children. But, unless our parents taught us about their presence, most of us completely forget about our angels by the time we reached puberty. Your parents were probably inclined to tell you that it was 'just your imagination' when you reported the awareness of one of your angels as a child. Fortunately this trend is changing as more adults come to experience angelic presence as truth and help to keep this knowledge alive in their children.

Over the years I have received many wonderful gifts from my angels. They have helped me overcome obstacles and taught me very simple techniques to make my life more meaningful and happier. But the most important things my angels have shown me is how easy it is to make them a part of my life — to communicate and interact with them, to access their wisdom

and loving energy, and therefore live a more fulfilled and fulfilling life.

Once you have met and talked with your own magical guides, your life will never be the same.

PART ONE

PREPARING TO MEET YOUR ANGELS

How can you connect with the angelic realm?

In the same way that our imagination helps us bring something to life, it also helps us to connect with the levels of life that we cannot perceive with our five physical senses. There is so much more going on around us than what our eyes can see or our ears can hear.

Your imagination is the *bridge*, the vital link we all have, between our physical and non-physical worlds. Without your imagination you could never imagine talking to a true angel, you would never even think to see one. Imagination is creation, and the act of creation engages and interests your angels; it brings them closer to you in order to communicate with them in reality.

Try this simple exercise to open up your vital link to the angels.

Exercising your imagination

When someone says they can't visualise things very well, especially something that is not normally seen, like an angel, I ask them to imagine something more common to their everyday experience. This exercise is designed to help you get used to using your imagination.

Find a quiet space where you can sit or lie comfortably.

Close your eyes and sit quietly for a minute or two and allow yourself to visualise a lovely red apple, all shiny, plump and fresh. Notice the texture of the skin and the flecks of varying colour. Allow your mind's eye to enjoy this attractive image.

By doing this exercise you are activating your mind's eye, which interprets information and guidance into pictures. It doesn't matter whether you practice picturing an apple, some flowers or something else familiar to you like your favourite pet, it's all about activating your 'inner' vision.

Once you become accustomed to this practice you can challenge yourself by trying to imagine an angel, allowing your imagination to create an angel that is unique to you.

Imagining Your Angel

Find a quiet space where you can sit or lie comfortably.

Close your eyes and sit quietly for a few moments, and give yourself permission to imagine an angel.

Imagine this angel however you would like he/she to be. It won't matter if you have never 'seen' an angel before as you determine exactly what your angel looks like.

Maybe your angel will look like the traditional representation with big golden wings and a halo, or like a small cherub, or even a ball of pure silver light. There is no right way or wrong way to imagine an angel.

Let the image play gently in your mind. Do not try to grab onto any particular image. Welcome them all as they come and allow them gently to fade away.

Take pleasure in this simple exercise and let it be fun. Repeat it for a few minutes whenever you like.

Your imagination is a very valuable tool. Use it, exercise it, treasure and respect it because your imagination is your vital link to encouraging your angels to communicate with you.

Now you have imagined what your angel looks like you will be less fearful of seeing and interacting with a real angel. Now is the time to prepare yourself to communicate with the angels who are watching over you.

To communicate with your angels you need to make yourself as open to the spirit realm as possible, and the best way to do this is to reactivate and strengthen your 'Angel Antenna'.

Your Angel Antenna

Your Angel Antenna is like a beam or column of light that connects you to your heavenly guidance. It flows from the centre of the Universe into the crown of your head and through the whole of your body, right down into the centre of the Earth. It is the instrument that you will activate and use in the receiving of all your Divine Guidance from your angels, whether it comes in words, sounds, pictures, or as feelings.

Your antenna is already active to a certain degree, because your antenna plays a vital role in the distribution of the life force energies that flow into and around your body. It also connects you to the highest possible level of your angels — the connection point or junction between Heaven and Earth, a living, breathing receiver, ready to bring the messages of angels into your world.

Your Angel Antenna is an invaluable tool, the conduit for all the inspiration and information your angels have to give you. Here are some simple tips on how to clear and strengthen it to ensure the angels can connect to you properly and don't get 'fuzzy' reception.

ACTIVATING YOUR ANGEL ANTENNA

Settle yourself comfortably and relax. Close your eyes when you are ready to begin.

Imagine a beam of golden-white light travelling down to you from way up in the cosmos. Picture it travelling through the heavens directly from the angelic realm, making a beeline for you here on planet Earth.

Let the golden-white light shine onto the top of your head and then down through your head and neck, and then through the length of your body. This beam of light will be

cylindrical in shape, like a pipe or a tube and flow through the centre of your body in front of your spine.

Once the light reaches the base of your spine let it branch out and continue to flow down through both your hips and legs, passing through the upper legs, knees, lower legs and ankles to the soles of your feet.

From there, picture the golden-white light reforming into one branch again and flowing down through the floor and into the Earth, all the way to her core. Connecting your antenna to the Earth's core is very important because it brings your divine guidance into your everyday, physical life and helps you feel more centred.

Now you have the Universal light flowing through you from top to bottom, connecting through you from the heavens to the core of the Earth.

Next, imagine a beautiful, rich red light, the colour of a fine red wine, travelling back up towards you from the Earth. While the golden-white light from above is vibrant and energising, the red light from the Earth is warm, comforting and nurturing.

Feel it flow up through the soles of your feet and move all the way back up through your body — legs, hips, core of your body and head — until it flows up and out through the top of your head and into Heaven.

Keep breathing deeply and steadily, giving yourself a few moments to become reacquainted with this flow of energy.

After a few minutes slowly open your eyes and reacquaint yourself with your surroundings. Your antenna will continue to be open and ready to receive any angelic communication.

Repeat this exercise whenever you want to prepare to speak with your angels.

PART TWO

COMMUNICATING WITH YOUR ANGELS

Once you have opened up the channels to contact your angels, the next step is to do some simple exercises that can help you to communicate directly with them.

The first and simplest exercise is to open yourself up to whatever message your angels have to give you.

Writing to your angels

The angels are always willing to listen to your problems or concerns and one of the best ways to connect with them is the same way you can communicate with any friend — simply write them a letter.

You can write a letter to your angels whenever you wish, as

they are always there watching over you. Don't feel that you have to hold back or be 'nice' either; you cannot offend your angels, they have literally seen it all before! The main thing is to be clear about why you are writing to them and genuine about your desire for a solution or situation you want to create.

Sometimes you may think that your letter has gone unanswered, but the angels always hear you and respond when it is necessary. Sometimes the angels know you just needed to express your feelings and don't need anything done. Other times they will allow you the time and space to uncover your own solutions rather than 'butting in'. Remember the angels help manifest in many ways, not always the way we would expect.

WRITING A LETTER TO YOUR ANGELS

Requirements: A quiet location where you can sit and write comfortably

Writing paper

Envelope

Pen or pencil

Time required: 10 to 30 minutes

Set a nice mood if you like by lighting a candle and putting on some relaxing music, then sit at a desk or table with a pen and paper. On the top of the paper simply write 'Dear Angels', then start writing.

Be as clear as you can. Put everything you want to say in your letter — don't hold back. Angels can cope with everything, no matter how impolite or overwhelming you may think it to be.

Once you have finished writing, put your letter in an envelope and address it to your angels — wherever you think they may live.

Ask your angels how they would like you to send the letter and go with the first impulse that comes to mind, whether it be burying it, burning it, casting it out onto the ocean or even putting it into the post.

Once you have completed and sent the letter do not dwell on the situation or the possible solution. Trust that all that can be done is being done by your angels. If you have asked for help, wait for the results to manifest for you without anxiety.

VALIDATION

The signs that your letter has been received by your divine friends are as varied as angels themselves. You might notice a feather in an unusual place, or the words of a song you have heard a hundred times may suddenly strike you as important.

The responses are often very subtle and you may miss them at first. The main thing is that you trust that the letter is doing its work.

Even when your problems are serious or your situation is dire, your angels will often bring a solution to you that is humorous or light-hearted; this is not flippancy, but rather an acknowledgement that we can achieve a lot more when we are joyous and relaxed as opposed to anxious or grim.

Write your letter, send it and then relax. You will be prompted to take the next step when it is required.

STAYING IN TOUCH WITH YOUR ANGELS

Once you have started communicating with your angels, remember to keep in touch. Getting to know your angels is a lovely process. You don't just have to contact your angels when you have a problem. You may just like to say hello to them each morning, or ask them to reveal more information about themselves to you, such as their name.

Make time to sit and commune with your angels, or contemplate them as you are drifting off to sleep. Your angels want to have a closer relationship with you, so tell them about yourself, your life, how you feel and what you dream of. It's all about getting reacquainted with a long lost friend; there is a lot of catching up to do, so don't hold back.

My friend Hannah kept asking her angel for his name and didn't receive an answer. In frustration she rang me and said, 'maybe he doesn't want to tell me his name' and then she went off to work.

That day in the office the name Daniel kept coming to her from many different directions. She was introduced to someone called Daniel, two customer enquiries that she had to deal with were from people named Daniel and then finally, as she was driving home, the car in front of her in the slow-moving, peak hour traffic had a customised number plate with the letters DAN on it. She finally got it and laughed about it all the way home.

Your angels will find all sorts of interesting and creative ways to communicate with you and to help you to develop your faith in their presence. Their messages can come to you in any way, shape or form, so be observant and don't be surprised if a song you have heard a thousand times suddenly holds new meaning for you, or people keep mentioning similar ideas or themes to you in their conversation, or the headline on the next magazine or newspaper you pick up makes sense to you in a very personal way. Your angels will use whatever means are at hand — it's up to you to pay attention.

Once you are used to talking to your angels you may feel ready to actually meet one.

PART THREE

MEETING YOUR ANGELS

In my experience it is a rare person who isn't at least a little bit intrigued by the idea of meeting one of their angels. Some people already have a strong belief about the existence of their unseen friends, others have felt a loving presence around them before, particularly during a difficult time in their lives, but few have ever actually seen their angel manifest in front of them.

Meeting an angel is an amazing experience and one that is available to all of us, no matter how 'holy' we think we are. Each person has an angel watching over them, sometimes more than one, and getting to know them can be a very rewarding and uplifting experience.

The following exercise is simple, effective and a great way to meet with your angels.

MEETING ONE OF YOUR ANGELS

Requirements: A quiet place where you can sit or lie comfortably

Pen and notebook or journal

Time required: 10 to 20 minutes

Sit or lie down somewhere that you can be comfortable, take the phone off the hook, put the 'do not disturb' sign out — anything you need to ensure you won't be interrupted.

Place your pen and notebook within reach. Now close your eyes and take a moment to consider your intention, the reason you are doing this exercise — to meet one of your angels.

Imagine yourself travelling up into the sky, floating or flying. You leave behind your room and fly up through the sky, going higher and higher. Imagine the clouds as you pass them by, feeling happy, free and full of excited anticipation.

Soon you have risen so far that you begin to leave the Earth's atmosphere and are moving out into space.

Picture yourself going past our beautiful moon and out past the planets in our solar system such as Venus, Jupiter, Neptune and Pluto. Make your journey as colourful and interesting as you like; there is no need to rush. Stop and study the awesome and colourful rings of Saturn or marvel at the comets and asteroids as they glide on by.

When you feel ready, allow yourself to come to a stop and to simply float or hover in space with stars and planets moving slowly around you.

Look straight ahead of you into the distance and see a small but very bright point of light. Let this light come closer and closer towards you. It travels with great speed and accuracy, all the while becoming larger.

As you watch, a form begins to reveal itself to you; there is nothing you have to do other than just observe. Just relax and allow your angel to come to you. Be receptive and welcoming, and notice whatever shows up.

In your mind's eye let the image of your angel be shown

to you and keep asking for more information. It is perfectly acceptable to ask as many questions as you like, such as 'are you male or female?', 'what do you look like?' and 'what is your name?', especially if they are not very visual at this time.

When you feel that you have spent enough time reuniting with your friend you can then make your journey back to Earth, this time with your angel by your side.

Make your journey back logical and sequential, coming back the same way you went out, then returning to the country, city, town, suburb, street, home or building, and then finally the room you set out from. Affirm to yourself the present place and time; for example, your street address and the date. Breathe

deeply, wriggle your fingers and toes, feel the weight of your body in the chair, and then open your eyes. You are back where you started with your angel now there beside you. You may physically see them, or just feel their warm, loving presence, but be assured they are there and you have strongly connected with them.

Normally, you will meet just one angel each time you make this trip, but it is possible to be greeted by two or more. There are no rules, so be open to surprises and trust yourself and what you are being shown.

The Angel Resolution

Once you have met your angel they are much easier to connect with and can often offer you much more specific help.

One way your angel can do this is to help mediate problems for you by allowing you to connect with other people through the calming influence of the angelic realm. This type of conflict resolution is called an Angel or Angelic Resolution. It can be a very effective way to resolve problems with those people you find it difficult or impossible to communicate with here in the Earthly realm.

Angels are wonderful mediators and this lovely technique can help you ease emotionally challenging situations without putting yourself or the other person's feelings at risk.

An Angel Resolution is effective because the angels help you communicate, not only with words and thoughts, but also with feelings. Angel Resolutions can also be a great help when the person you want to communicate with lives far away. Phone calls, letters and emails are notorious for being open to misinterpretation over long distances and/or when you haven't seen the person for quite some time.

So if you freeze at the idea of fronting up to a certain person with a request or a problem, if you know that your voice will shake, or your bottom lip will quiver, or that you are liable to burst into tears and forget half the things you wanted to say, don't feel bad. You are not being weak, you are simply being human.

That's where the angels can help. Through Angel Resolution they allow you to approach someone that you might even be afraid of, and get a positive result. It can turn supposed enemies into friends, intimidators into supporters, resolve issues with people who no longer belong in your life so you can let them go, and give you a sense of inner strength that you did not previously know you had.

The Angel Resolution was shown to me by my angels many years ago. It helps resolve situations by giving you the

opportunity to communicate with others at the level of the heart, and concentrate fully on your feelings and what you want to communicate.

Well, here's how to do it. Read the instructions carefully and keep it simple. The most important thing is that you are purely to express your true feelings honestly and ask for the outcome you most desire. It is most effective if you have already tried discussing your concern with

the person before asking the

angels to help you with the resolution. And remember this is not about blaming or accusing the other person, but giving you an opportunity to tell them honestly how you feel about their actions or words. It is about owning your own feelings on the matter and creating this chance to express them.

MEETING YOUR ANGELS 2
THE ANGEL RESOLUTION

Requirements: A quiet location where you can sit or lie comfortably

A clear intention

Time required: Approximately 10 to 15 minutes

First decide who it is you want to talk to and what your main topic will be.

Sit or lie somewhere quiet, comfortable and private, and close your eyes. Calm your mind and focus on your intention, including the outcome you would like to have happen as a result of this conversation.

Imagine your angel coming out of the ether towards you, taking your hand and leading you to the angelic realm where all is calm, peaceful and beautiful.

Imagine your angel leading the person you wish to talk to into this space. The angel then sits quietly apart from you as you welcome the person and you both make yourselves comfortable.

The angel's loving energy and calmness will help ensure that your anger, bitterness or other negative feelings towards this person do not stop you from communicating effectively.

Begin the resolution by clearly stating your topic, then tell the person everything you have not been able to tell them in real life. Imagine them sitting and listening to you respectfully and attentively; simply taking in what you are saying without reaction. Go into as much detail as you want and need. Say everything you need to say and get it all off your chest. This is your time to speak because you have created this opportunity to do it, so use it well.

When you are completely finished, be sure to then say what outcome you want — what you want this person to do or say

that will make you feel better and be able to move on from the disagreement or conflict.

Would you like an apology? How about a phone call from that person, or an offer to renew the friendship? Maybe you want to get back together with your partner and also had an apology to offer them during the conversation; or maybe it is a pay rise that you want. Make sure that your desired outcome is very clear.

After you have completely expressed your feelings about your side of the situation and been clear about the outcome you would like, you can then thank them for coming and hearing you, and politely ask them to leave. The other person does not reply or respond — remember, they are a being of free will — so it is not for you to try to imagine what they might say at this time. This meeting was initiated by you and was your opportunity to talk.

Once the person has 'left', turn to your angel and thank them for creating this aura of peace and allowing you to communicate on this angelic realm. Then allow them to gently disappear as you slowly come back to Earth and open your eyes.

If you wish, jot down the details of who you spoke to, what you said and what outcome you requested.

After conducting an Angel Resolution most people report that they feel a sense of relief or lightness because they have finally found a constructive way to release something that they have been carrying around inside themselves for a while.

Now it is up to the other person to respond and time for you to let go, because you cannot control them. The best thing you can do now is to forget all about it and get on with your life.

If you believe that you are dealing with someone who is particularly stubborn or resistant then you may have the same or similar conversation with them a total of three times. My angels taught me a 'three strikes you're out' policy with Angel Resolutions. After all you can only try to communicate with people so many times before realising they simply don't wish to change. So it is recommended that if you try an Angel Resolution with the same person three times and still get no response, then it is time to accept that they are simply not interested in your point of view, and move on.

Sometimes the response will come to you in ways that you hadn't imagined. You may well get the apology that you wanted, for example, but it may come in the form of a letter or card, or through a third party, rather than in person or on the phone as you might have expected. Understand that you are learning a new way of communicating with people, and like all new skills this one will also benefit you more with practice, so be patient with yourself and allow space for your desired outcome to happen in miraculous ways.

And remember you can use the Angel Resolution for good things too. If someone in your life that you adore is a bit prickly or difficult to get close to, or you feel a bit shy then you can also go to the angelic realm to tell that person that you love them.

PART FOUR

MESSAGES FROM THE ANGELS

As you communicate more with your angels you will be amazed at the wonderful ideas and techniques they can share with you. Many of these messages you will feel compelled to share with others, as angels are concerned with the whole human race and many of the ideas they share with you could be helpful for many.

I have experienced many of these kinds of messages, some of which were perfect to share with specific individuals who were going through particular trials or difficulties in their lives, and others which were perfect to share with anyone who wished to listen.

The following exercises are three universal messages that I believe can benefit everyone, so my angels and I are pleased to share them with you, just as you will be pleased to share some of your angel's guidance with your loved ones, friends and family.

THE ANGEL HEART BALANCE

Angels wants us to be happy and have the life we want, but often we don't know what to ask for. The following exercise was given to me by my angels to help me determine and then create my true heart's desires.

THE ANGEL HEART BALANCE

Requirements: A place to sit or lie down comfortably

Your journal and a pen

Anything you like to create a pleasant atmosphere

Time required: 10 to 15 minutes

How often should I do this? Once a week or whenever you feel like it

This exercise can be done sitting up or lying down. Make sure you are comfortable, relaxed and attentive.

Consider your intention to experience and enjoy connecting your heart to your angels.

Now focus on the following three areas or zones in your body — the heart zone in the centre of your chest, the solar plexus area which is in the centre of your midriff, and your abdomen, just below your navel. Imagine a figure 8 connecting these three zones, with the solar plexus in the centre at the point where the figure 8 crosses over. Trace this figure 8 over your own body with your fingertips if you like to get a feel for where it sits, coming up from your abdomen, crossing over at the solar plexus, looping up and around through your heart and then back down through the solar plexus again in the other direction, returning to the abdomen and so on, in a continuous flow.

Imagine that a stream or tube of constantly moving energy is flowing around this figure 8, pulsing up and down between these three points of its own accord. You may even feel the energy as it moves through you.

Rest the palms of your hands on these points. Whichever of them you feel drawn to is fine. Move one of your hands to the other area from time to time whenever you wish. Keep both of your palms on any two of the areas for the duration of the balance.

Take a minute or two to notice what qualities you feel and how the energy is flowing around the figure 8. Don't try to analyse what you pick up, just focus on what you feel or sense.

Let your hands be the vehicles for a healing energy and light that flows down to you from the Universe. Picture a beautiful, rich orange light flowing from your palms directly into the areas you are touching.

Send this energy and light in and feel it flow up and down through the entire figure 8, clearing away any dull colour or blockages, and getting the energy moving more consistently, or calming it down to a nice gentle flow. Stay with that for at least five minutes or until you feel that the energy is moving well and that the colour is lovely and bright.

Keep breathing deeply, moving your hands between these three points and visualising the orange energy and light flowing into them, and the figure 8, through your hands. If you sense that the bright healing colour is something other than orange that is absolutely fine; whatever colour comes to you is the colour to work with at this time and may vary from session to session.

Imagine this beautiful energy flowing up and down through this figure 8 in your body. Feel your solar plexus becoming calm and balanced, your heart becoming clear and confident, and the creativity from your abdominal area stirring and coming back to life. Stay with it until you feel you are glowing from within!

When you are ready, take your hands away and rest them by your sides, then picture yourself being surrounded by a beautiful cocoon of silver, gold or white light.

If you wish you may make a few notes in your journal about what else you noticed during this exercise. Write down anything you feel you might like to refer back to in the future.

I normally feel great after doing the Angel Heart Balance and I'm sure you will too.

PART FIVE

Heavenly Bliss!

A reasonable level of health and fitness is the greatest asset you can have. The angels have shared a lovely exercise that can make you feel better and more motivated to increase your level of fitness in other ways too.

The exercise is called Heavenly Bliss and is a simple process taught to me by my angels a few years ago. I often use it when I feel tired and need to refresh myself. It is a great treatment to use in stress situations also, like studying for exams, and is great for tired eyes after staring at a computer screen for hours. The bubbly golden light will also lift your mood, so if you have a tendency towards melancholy, feel a bit low or have a habit of looking on the pessimistic side of life, then the Heavenly Bliss treatment will provide an excellent pep-up. It is cleansing and revitalising on all levels — mental, emotional, physical and spiritual — so treat yourself to a little angelic champagne any time you like.

Creating Heavenly Bliss

Requirements: A place to sit comfortably

Optional: Gentle music, a candle, incense

Anything that helps you create a pleasant atmosphere

Time required: 5 to 10 minutes

How often should I do this? Daily if you wish as a regular treatment to boost energy, provide mild relief from certain ailments, or whenever you feel you need it.

Sit comfortably with the soles of your feet flat on the floor, your hands resting in your lap or by your side. Breathe deeply and consider your intention to give yourself a lovely angelic pick-me-up.

Take a moment to imagine the centre of the heavens, whatever that may look like to you, surrounded by the wonders of the universe. See the planets and swirling galaxies fading away into the infinite distance.

Visualise a stream of this bubbly, pale gold energy and light flowing down from the centre of Heaven and coming gently down towards you and onto the top of your head. Imagine this light flowing into your whole body through your crown and over the surface of your body as well.

Picture this light bubbling and gurgling through every part of you, in between every cell and fibre of your physical form. If you have a headache or tired eyes then you can intend more of

the golden light to go to those areas to clear away the fatigue and stress. Ask the light to go to the areas of your body and energy field (aura) that need it most.

Continue to breathe in a deep and relaxed manner. Keep your mind gently focused on the light as it makes its way from the heavens towards, and then through and around you. Ask that it wash away any negative or superfluous worries or thoughts that may be weighing you down, and then let it flow out through and over your legs and feet into the floor.

Imagine our beautiful Mother Earth absorbing it all and drawing it all away. Feel the golden light with its refreshing bubbles soaking into the earth beneath you. Stay with the process until you feel the last of the light drain away and when you are ready, open your eyes.

If you wish, you may also like to surround yourself in a cocoon of white energy and light, or any other colour of your choice. Once your Heavenly Bliss is over you will feel refreshed and ready to get on with or continue your day.

The meaning of life

My angels have told me over and over that happiness is the actual meaning and purpose of our lives. It is, in fact, why we are here. More surprisingly the angels want me to know that happiness comes from within, not from what we own or who we are with — but by who we are. So you could say that learning to be happy within yourself is the purpose of your life and in turn, it is the main thing that the angels will guide you towards.

Some people believe that a sense of meaning and purpose in life can only come to you once you have done something notable, or found that special thing you are supposed to do or person you are supposed to be with. But the angels love us and think we are important because of who we are, not just what we do.

The angels want us to know the simple things in life can bring us the greatest feelings of contentment. Many things can bring happiness, meaning and purpose into your life, so it pays to focus on small victories. If something or someone is in your life regularly then they are most likely put there by angels because they help you or give you information in some way.

HEAVEN ON EARTH

Creating meaning, purpose and happiness in your life

Requirements: Your journal and a pen

Peace and quiet

Optional: Soft music, a candle, incense

Anything you like to create a pleasant atmosphere

Time required: 10 to 15 minutes

How often should I do this? At least once

This can be a great exercise to do on an anniversary of some kind like your birthday, or New Year's Eve.

Write down the things that have given your life meaning

and purpose in the past, and what gives your life meaning and purpose now. Be sure to note down all the people, pets, activities, experiences and even possessions.

Review and add to your list any time you want to feel inspired.

EPILOGUE

Honouring your angels

Now that you have started to communicate more effectively with your angels you will start to see that their intentions for you are always for you to live the best, happiest, most inspiring life possible.

Angels are the source of inspiration and creativity, and by meeting and talking to them you will find that suddenly you will be seeing your life in a completely different way. Those parts of your life that are not fulfilling will suddenly seem impossible to endure, while those things that make your heart sing and your passions rise will become more alluring.

Do not ignore this. Honour this gift that your angels are giving you and follow the path they are able to guide you on — the one that leads to a more interesting, rewarding and inspiring existence.

That is your angel's wish for you.

Blessings

BelindaGrace

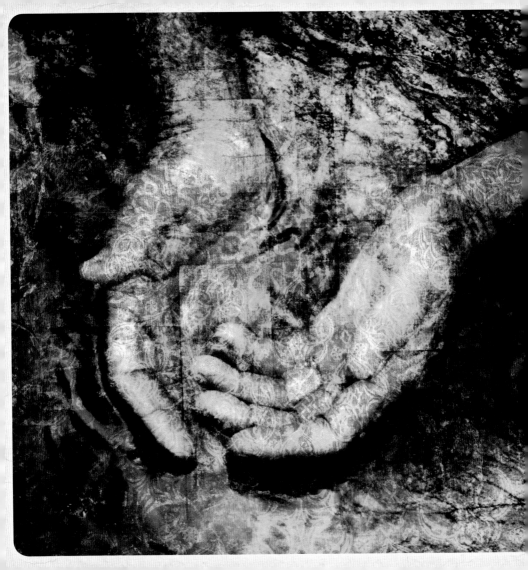